i

Contents

Abstract

Many papers and reports have been written on Al Qaeda and the western principles of war. Government agencies and universities throughout the world work hard to analyze the background of Al Qaeda to better understand the organization and where its next strike might occur. At the same time, theorists and academics debate whether the principles of war debated since the time of Clausewitz still apply to the modern battles that the west faces against Al Qaeda. Very little work has been done combining these two topics to determine if Al Qaeda has unique principles of war and if so, what can be done about them. This paper defines what a principle of war is and then analyzes Al Qaeda's principles of war by comparing them to the accepted western principles of war as stated in the latest version of the US Army Field Manual 3-0 Operations. It also looks at what can be done, once Al Qaeda's principles of war are determined, to gain the upper hand in the Global War on Terror.

INTRODUCTION

Since the 9/11 attacks against America, there have been more articles written on Al Qaeda than can be easily counted. This is not unexpected, as members of the U.S. government and other experts worldwide are trying to get inside the mind of the organization to determine what its next step will be. Each agency or scholar involved in this research and study has an idea regarding Al Qaeda; what its goals are, how it is structured, where its next attack will be, and how best to defeat it. What seems to be an abundance of talk and writing is actually necessary to provide the decision makers with as much information and potential solutions as possible. It is in this overwhelming amount of information where the next move in the global battle will be found, and these efforts need to continue.

Another area that has been thoroughly researched recently is the principles of war. Soon after the U.S. led overthrow of the Taliban in Afghanistan, the Office of Force Transformation at the Pentagon began asking questions concerning the principles of war and their validity. "In late 2002…we asked whether the traditional principles of war had changed. That, in turn, led to other questions. Was the very concept of principles of war still relevant to warfare in the twenty-first century? What, then, to make of the list of principles embedded in our fundamental service doctrines since the 1920s?"[1] These and other similar questions have since been debated by experts throughout the government in an attempt to find a better way for waging war.

What is striking is the distinct lack of research and writing on a synthesis of these two topics, Al Qaeda and its principles of war. Many authors have opinions on what the principles of war are from the United States' perspective and they have proposed different principles of war that we should follow in our approach to fighting Al Qaeda. Few, however,

---

[1] Anthony D. McIvor, ed., *Rethinking the Principles of War* (Annapolis, MD: Naval Institute Press, 2005), xiv.

have attempted to determine Al Qaeda's principles of war. Are they different than "traditional" western principles of war? Are they different than the proposed new western principles of war to be used in a counterinsurgency? Their tactics and techniques certainly differ on the battlefield, and they do not follow any established rules on the conduct of war such as the Geneva Convention, so why should their principles of war not be different on an operational or strategic level?

In truth, it appears that Al Qaeda's principles of war have some similarities to those of their western enemies, such as security and objective, but there are also some distinct differences, the biggest one being a principle of ideology. It is these differences that have caused our military problems thus far in our battle against Al Qaeda, and what it has morphed into, Al Qaeda and the Associated Movement (AQAM). It is only by studying these differences, discussing them, and breaking down what they are that we can eventually understand that they are not playing by the same rules, either tactically or operationally, and that we need to approach this worldwide battle from their perspective if we hope to eventually be successful.

To approach this problem, the principles of war have to be defined and their affect on one's approach to war must be determined. Next the current "traditional" or western principles of war must be used as a baseline to define Al Qaeda's principles of war and show how they differ. Finally, these differences must be studied to find the most effective way to approach this unique battle against a worldwide movement of terror and violence.

WHAT ARE PRINCIPLES OF WAR?

Countless military historians and theorists have attempted to quantify exactly what it takes to be successful in war. Officers at military war colleges and students of military history throughout civilian universities then spend hours studying these theories of war in an attempt to apply them to today's fight. These theories have evolved over time into what are typically referred to as principles of war.

The principles of war are a hotly debated topic these days, with some people claiming that we need to change the principles of war to keep up with the rapidly changing wars we are facing in Iraq and Afghanistan while others state that the whole idea of a principle of war is a flawed concept.[2] Still others feel that the principles of war are just fine the way they are and that the application of these principles is what needs to change to keep up with today's wars.[3] There are many articles and papers available debating what the western principles of war should be, but the accepted principles from U.S. Army doctrine are what will be compared to Al Qaeda's principles. To start with, this problem needs to be broken down by determining the definition of the word principle itself, which can be just as contentious as the status of the principles of war.

If you enter the word "principle" into the website *dictionary.com*, results from nine different dictionaries are displayed. Many entries define a principle as a basic law to be followed while other definitions state that it is a starting point or a guideline from which other discussions stem. According to Webster's Revised Unabridged Dictionary a principle is, "A fundamental truth; a comprehensive law or doctrine, from which others are derived, or

---

[2] Phillip S. Meilinger, "New Principles of War," *Armed Forces Journal*, January 2009, 16; and Thomas X. Hammes, "Rethinking the Principles of War: The Future of Warfare" in *Rethinking the Principles of War*, ed. Anthony D. McIvor (Annapolis, MD: Naval Institute Press, 2005), 263.
[3] Raymond E. Bell Jr, Brig Gen, "The Validity of the Principles of War," *Army* 57, no. 2 (Feb 2007).

on which others are founded; a general truth; an elementary proposition; a maxim; an axiom; a postulate."[4] This definition would imply that a principle is a rule that when followed will lead to achievement of a desired outcome. As the saying goes, however, in war the enemy gets a vote. He will also be striving for victory and he will be using his own version of the principles in an attempt to win the fight. Sticking strictly to the published principles of war could make a military predictable and, therefore, vulnerable.

The principles of war, and how they should be used, are not a problem to be taken lightly. Carl von Clausewitz, arguably the most influential military theoretician in history, even struggled with the definition of the principles of war. His writings, which are attempts to define the nature of war, describe it as a duel, a wrestling match, and a chameleon. War is constantly changing based on the enemy's actions and the fog and friction of battle. To deal with this, guidelines are needed from which the commander can use judgment to depart from. He believed that "[A] principle is also a law for action, but not in its formal, definitive meaning; it represents only the spirit and the sense of a law; in cases where the diversity of the real world cannot be contained within the rigid form of law, the application of principle allows for greater latitude of judgment. Cases to which principle cannot be applied must be settled by judgment; principle thus becomes essentially a support, or lodestar, to the man responsible for action."[5] Antulio Echevarria also credits Clausewitz as stating that "one must grasp the 'meaning' of the principles rather than treat them as 'rigid rules'."[6]

Clausewitz also states:

---

[4] Webster's Revised Unabridged Dictionary. MICRA, Inc. 28 Apr. 2009.
[5] James J. Schneider, "Agents of Change: Transforming the Principles of War for the 21st Century," *Army* 56, no. 7 (Jul 2006): 28.
[6] Antulio J. Echevarria II. "Principles of War or Principles of Battle?" in *Rethinking the Principles of War*, ed Anthony D. McIvor, (Annapolis, MD: Naval Institute Press, 2005), 61.

4

These principles, though the result of long thought and continuous study of the history of war, have none the less been drawn up hastily, and thus will not stand severe criticism in regard to form…These principles, therefore, will not so much give complete instruction to Your Royal Highness, as they will stimulate and serve as a guide for your own reflections.[7]

Put simply, the principles of war are the basic building blocks or fundamental truths that, when used in combination with one another in a manner based on the enemy being fought, will lead to victory. They are not a checklist that must be followed; rather they are a jumping off point from which successful military leaders will diverge. As Clausewitz put it, "Theory leaves it to the military leader, however, to act according to his own courage, according to his spirit of enterprise, and his self-confidence."[8]

WHAT ARE THE WESTERN PRINCIPLES OF WAR?

What then, are the western principles of war, and do we need to change them to meet the new style of threats that we are facing? According to Major Walter Piatt in his 1999 monograph titled *Do the Principles of War Still Apply*, "the Army claims to have adopted [the current] principles in 1921 from the work of British Major General J.F.C. Fuller."[9] Little has changed in these principles since the U.S. Army first published them into doctrine, but their presence in doctrine was a contentious battle in and of itself. Several times throughout their history, the principles were removed, based on debates of whether principles should even be stated and if they are stated, which ones should be chosen.[10]

The latest version of the Army Operations Manual (now called FM 3-0 Operations) was published in February 2008, and it includes principles of war much like those first

---

[7] Carl von Clausewitz, "Principles of War" in *Roots of Strategy Book 2*, (Harrisburg, PA: Stackpole Books, 1987), 315.
[8] Ibid., 318.
[9] Walter E. Piatt, Major, *Do the Principles of War Still Apply?* School of Advanced Military Studies Research Paper (Ft Leavenworth, KS: 1999), 3.
[10] Ibid., 19.

postulated by Fuller after World War I. The principles are listed in Appendix A of the Field Manual, and they now include three new principles, called principles of operations. "In addition to [the] nine principles, JP 3-0 adds three principles of operations – perseverance, legitimacy, and restraint. Together with the principles of war, these twelve make up the principles of joint operations."[11]

According to FM 3-0, "the nine principles of war represent the most important nonphysical factors that affect the conduct of operation at the strategic, operational, and tactical levels…[they] are not a checklist. While they are considered in all operations, they do not apply in the same way to every situation."[12] In order to form a baseline for comparison between the western principles of war and those that Al Qaeda currently follows, the rest of this section will be dedicated to reviewing the twelve accepted western principles.

OBJECTIVE – "Direct every military operation toward a clearly defined, decisive, and attainable objective."

OFFENSIVE – "Seize, retain, and exploit the initiative."

MASS – "Concentrate the effects of combat power at the decisive place and time."

ECONOMY OF FORCE – "Allocate minimum essential combat power to secondary efforts."

MANEUVER – "Place the enemy in a disadvantageous position through the flexible application of combat power."

UNITY OF COMMAND – "For every objective, ensure unity of effort under one responsible commander."

SECURITY – "Never permit the enemy to acquire an unexpected advantage."

---

[11] U.S. Army, *Operations*.Field Manual (FM) 3-0 (Washington D.C.: Department of the Army, February 2008), A-3.
[12] Ibid., A-1.

SURPRISE – "Strike the enemy at a time or place or in a manner for which he is unprepared."

SIMPLICITY – "Prepare clear, uncomplicated plans and clear, concise orders to ensure thorough understanding."

PERSEVERENCE – "Ensure the commitment necessary to attain the national strategic end state."

LEGITIMACY – "Develop and maintain the will necessary to attain the national strategic end state."

RESTRAINT – "Limit collateral damage and prevent the unnecessary use of force."[13]

Now that the principles of war, based on Army Field Manual 3-0 have been established, the process of investigating whether Al Qaeda uses similar principles of war can begin. It the differences between these principles that might provide us with another target that can be exploited to bring about a successful conclusion to this current war.

WHAT ARE AL QAEDA'S PRINCIPLES OF WAR?

At first glance, it seems that many of the western principles of war would also apply to Al Qaeda operations. There is no question that success in any endeavor, whether from a terrorist or counterinsurgent perspective, is based on knowing what the objective is and putting all efforts towards achieving that objective. It is also fairly obvious that surprise is a major aspect of Al Qaeda operations. At the same time, however, their approach to mass and unity of command are almost completely the opposite of western principles. They also add a new principle to the list, that of an ideology fueling their war. First we will consider the principles of war that are similar between Al Qaeda and the western world.

---

[13] Ibid., A-1 - A-3.

Al Qaeda's stated strategic objective is "a world-wide Islamic caliphate where the only law is sharia or Islamic law."[14] In a letter to Abu Musab al Zarqawi, Ayman Al Zawahiri stated "If our intended goal in this age is the establishment of a caliphate in the manner of the Prophet, and if we expect to establish its state predominantly -- according to how it appears to us -- in the heart of the Islamic world, then your efforts and sacrifices -- God permitting -- are a large step directly towards that goal."[15] The leadership has determined what their strategic objective is, and they have established operational level objectives which they believe will help them get there. Their operational objectives include the expulsion of American forces from Iraq and the Middle East, establishing an Islamic emirate in Iraq, extending the jihad started in Iraq to the secular countries throughout the Middle East, and finally defeating Israel.[16] It is evident throughout the writings and recordings of the leadership of Al Qaeda that these objectives drive everything they do.

The next principle that is similar between western forces and Al Qaeda is the principle of surprise. The ability to strike the enemy at a time and in a manner for which he is not prepared is the obvious modus operandi of terrorists throughout history. Unable to face the U.S. military in a set piece battle and succeed, Al Qaeda has to rely on surprise in order to gain the advantage. The hijacking and use of four civilian airliners as weapons came as a complete surprise to people throughout the world. The United States was unprepared for anything like this attack because of the manner in which it was accomplished.

Security for Al Qaeda is closely related to surprise. Just as the United States military protects its secrets and plans from the enemy in order to achieve surprise, Al Qaeda does the

---

[14] Brian M. Drinkwine, *Serpent in Our Garden: Al Qa'ida and the Long War*, Strategic Studies Institute, (Carlisle, PA: Strategic Studies Institute, Jan 2009), 1.
[15] *Letter from Zawahiri to Zarqawi*, Published by the Office of the Director of National Intelligence, in *In the Eyes of Your Enemy: An Al-Qaeda Compendium*, (Newport, RI: Strategy and Policy Department, 2008).
[16] Ibid.

same. According to Al Qaeda's by-laws translated in 2008, "secrecy is of utmost importance and is vital to our operations. We shall only reveal what we absolutely must reveal."[17] Another way they maintain security was seen in the months leading up to the 9/11 attack, when members of the Hamburg contingent of terrorists worked hard to avoid the appearance that they were involved in planning an attack on the United States. "…[T]hey distanced themselves from conspicuous extremists…they also changed their appearance and behavior. [Mohammad] Atta wore western clothing, shaved his beard, and no longer attended extremist mosques."[18] These efforts successfully kept the terrorists and their plans out of the hands of western governments.

Remaining out of the spotlight of western governments helps Al Qaeda follow the principle of the offensive. The leadership seeks to gain and retain the offensive by hitting the United States and its allies throughout the world at a time of their choosing. By posing this worldwide threat, Al Qaeda places western governments into a situation where they are reacting and unable to seize the initiative. This is also an area where Al Qaeda made an error. By putting a stake in the ground in Iraq and Afghanistan and stating that this fight was going to be the central front of their fight against the United States, they took away their advantage. Knowing that the fight is going to occur in Iraq and Afghanistan allows the U.S. to focus our efforts in these two theaters while still maintaining awareness of other areas of potential operations. This one piece of information makes it much more challenging for Al Qaeda to seize the offensive by striking where and when they please.

When these strikes do take place, Al Qaeda is very good at following the principle of economy of force. The Planes Operation is a perfect example of using the minimum force

---

[17] Harmony Project, "AFGP-2002-600048," in *Harmony and Disharmony*, 2.
[18] The National Commission on Terrorist Attacks Upon the United States, *The 9/11 Commission Report*, (New York: W.W. Norton and Co, 2004) 167.

necessary to accomplish the job. Al Qaeda was able to bring down the World Trade Center, hit the Pentagon, and potentially destroy the White House all while only losing 19 terrorists and at a minimum cost monetarily.[19] The leadership accepts that this is a long war and the more painful they can make it for the United States, the greater chance they have of succeeding.[20] To do so, they are unwilling to lose large numbers of their soldiers without taking out a larger number of targets.

This leads directly to the next principle that is similar between Al Qaeda and the western world, perseverance. Osama bin Laden and Al Qaeda are in this fight until the end. They are willing to do what it takes for as long as it takes to win. As stated by bin Laden himself on 19 January 2006, "We have been tolerant for 10 years in fighting the Soviet Union with our few weapons and we managed to drain their economy…We will remain patient in fighting you, god willing, until the one whose time has come dies first. We will not escape the fight as long as we hold our weapons in our hands."[21]

Al Qaeda's strategy is just that simple, outlast the United States. At the operational level, however, we start to see a divergence from the western principle of simplicity. Western countries are not willing to allow terrorists to openly plan attacks that will kill innocent civilians. Therefore the planning and preparations have to occur in secret, which greatly complicates things. Consider once again the Planes Operation. Al Qaeda had to get 19 terrorists on board four different planes headed to different locations, take control of those planes, and then crash them into four different buildings in two separate cities near

---

[19] Ibid.

[20] Osama bin Laden, *Speech from 30 October 2004*, in *In the Eyes of Your Enemy: An Al-Qaeda Compendium*, (Newport, RI: Strategy and Policy Department, 2008).

[21] Osama bin Laden, *Audio Tape from 19 January 2006*, in *In the Eyes of Your Enemy: An Al-Qaeda Compendium*, (Newport, RI: Strategy and Policy Department, 2008).

simultaneously. The idea of crashing aircraft into buildings is not a complicated idea, but the execution of that plan is where simplicity is lost.

The final principle that is similar between Al Qaeda and the traditional principles is maneuver; not necessarily the movement of armored columns in order to outflank the enemy, but in the selected application of combat power to put the enemy at a disadvantage. This is similar to Al Qaeda's ability to seize the offensive by striking when and where they want. It is impossible for western forces to be everywhere all the time. Therefore the minimum about of "maneuver" is required for Al Qaeda to put them on the defensive. By incorporating different groups into its organization, Al Qaeda is able to mount attacks throughout the world, introducing new threats and dangers to the equation, whether it is suicide bombers at checkpoints, or small boats laden with explosives attacking surface combatants.

The first two western principles of war that Al Qaeda does not follow are restraint and legitimacy. Restraint is obviously not a concern to Al Qaeda. "While the United States is bound in its conduct of war by both international conventions and its own codes of ethics, al Qaeda displays no such limitations, targeting noncombatants and other conventionally protected categories solely on the basis of their vulnerability."[22] According to Osama bin Laden's original Fatwa in 1998, "The ruling to kill the Americans and their allies – civilians and military – is an individual duty for every Muslim who can do it in any country in which it is possible to do it..."[23] Restraint is not even considered by Al Qaeda, much less as a principle of war.

---

[22]Hassan Mneimneh, "Seven Years Later: The Jihadist International," *American Enterprise Institute for Public Policy Research*, September 2008, 2.
[23] World Islamic Front, "Jihad Against Jews and Crusaders 23 Feb 1998," in *In the Eyes of Your Enemy: An Al-Qaeda Compendium*, (Newport, RI: Strategy and Policy Department, 2008).

At the same time, legitimacy does not apply to Al Qaeda for many of the same reasons. Legitimacy, according to the American Heritage dictionary means "being in compliance with the law; lawful."[24] One of Al Qaeda's stated objectives is to "topple Arab and Muslim regimes that are corrupt and apostate (anti-Islamic) and install fundamentalist Islamic rule through a single Muslim nation (Caliphate) that would strictly govern in accordance with the sharia (Islamic Law)."[25] If their goal is to overthrow established countries and their laws in order to create their own caliphate living under fundamentalist Islamic law, obviously they are not concerned with legitimacy in the eyes of those countries.

Unfortunately, there is little that the United States can do to take advantage of Al Qaeda's lack of restraint and legitimacy beyond what is already being done. They are terrorists, and killing innocents to incite panic is at the core of their tactics. "…Al Qaeda adheres to a wholesale rejection of the world order: where states, governments, and international organizations are deemed illegitimate."[26] If this is the case, what can be done? We cannot make them see that killing innocents is wrong, and if they want to overthrow the existing world order, then why should they care about being legitimate within its standards?

The final two Al Qaeda principles of war are where the major divergence lies from western principles of war. These areas are important to understanding the differences between the west and Al Qaeda and will provide some areas where friendly forces can focus their efforts in an attempt to defeat them. These principles are called dispersal of command and ideology, and both of them are related.

---

[24] *The American Heritage Dictionary of the English Language*, Fourth Edition, Houghton Mifflin Company, 2004.
[25] Drinkwine, "Serpent In Our Garden," 14.
[26] Mneimneh, "Seven Years Later," 1.

Dispersal of command describes the structure of Al Qaeda and how it spreads the organization out in order to prevent the enemy from massing its forces. They have created a network of terrorism by integrating groups throughout the world. These groups are bound by "a gripping sense of shared belonging, principles of fusion against an outside enemy, and a jihadist narrative so compelling that it amounts both to an ideology and a doctrine."[27]

Another way to look at the organization of Al Qaeda is to picture it like a fast food restaurant, most likely a franchise guided by rules from a headquarters, but able to act independently as long as it is moving towards the ultimate goal of making money:

> "Al Qaeda is not a cohesive organization with centralized governance. Instead it is a diffuse network of 'franchises'… The franchises offer allegiance to a global nominal charismatic leadership that, through direct involvement or through the endorsement of local initiatives, has an arbitrage function, redirecting resources – human and financial – in order to optimize impact and effect."[28]

Unlike your favorite restaurant though, this network can actually work against itself. The different groups, while all basically swearing loyalty to bin Laden and Al Qaeda's goal of overthrowing the existing world order in order to establish the caliphate, tend to approach the problem in their own way. Each individual group in the organization has what they believe to be the best approach to accomplishing their objectives. "The lack of institutional capacity for sustained action, inherent to the nature of the diffuse network, drastically limits the likelihood of al Qaeda translating its ultimate utopian (or dystopian) dream into reality, but the carnage and dislocation it has inflicted in recent years demonstrate amply that the problem cannot be reduced to one of law and order."[29]

---

[27] David Ronfeldt, "Al-Qaeda and its Affiliates: A Global Tribe Waging Segmental Warfare," *Rand Document # RP-1371*, 2007, 43.
[28] Mneimneh, "Seven Years Later," 1.
[29] Ibid., 2.

So if we accept the fact that the problem cannot be solved through law and order, we have to take a more aggressive approach to its defeat. This kind of organization cannot be defeated through the decapitation of its leadership or through random attacks such as arbitrarily stopping terrorists at our borders. "A small-world network resists fragmentation because of its dense interconnectivity. A significant fraction of nodes can be randomly removed without much impact on its integrity. [Instead], where a small-world network is vulnerable to targeted attack is at its hubs. If enough hubs are destroyed, the network breaks down into isolated, noncommunicating islands of nodes."[30]

Unfortunately for us, Al Qaeda has one last principle of war and this one is essential to its whole survival and continued existence as a movement. Al Qaeda's Salafi and jihad ideology are what holds it together and what will prove the most difficult piece to combat. "Salafis are Sunni Muslims who want to establish and govern Islamic states based solely on interpretation of the teachings of the Prophet and the Quran, and to abandon modern secular governments."[31] Jihadists are the violent extremists within the Salafi movement that feel that the only way to accomplish their goals is through violence and holy war.

This jihadist ideology is based on the interpretation and study of the Quran by Islamic clerics and scholars such as Sayyid Qutb who believed that the Islamic world was no longer Muslim because of the lack of sharia law. In order to return the world to true Islam, a group of pious Muslims must move to rid the world of all non-Islamic influences.[32] The words of the Quran, however, can be interpreted in different ways. What one scholar takes as a call to violence, another might read as something completely different. Members of Al Qaeda, "to

---

[30] Marc Sageman, *Understanding Terror Networks*, (Philadelphia: University of Pennsylvania Press, 2004), 140.
[31] Drinkwine, "Serpent In Our Garden," 6.
[32] Ibid., 8.

compensate for this potential pitfall…have instituted a 'maximalist' approach that always errs on the side of severity and austerity."[33] Their interpretation of the Quran from a violent perspective is the basis for the terrorist activities followed by Al Qaeda.

These interpretations of the Quran, added to the common belief that the world is working against Muslims, leads to the violent ideology upon which Al Qaeda was formed. They can then take this ideology and use it to recruit at mosques and universities worldwide. Part of this recruitment is convincing Muslims that they are obligated to fight against non-believers. This is where verses within the Quran that call for Muslims to fight against infidels, called war verses, come in. An example is, "Those who believe do battle for the cause of Allah; and those who disbelieve do battle for the cause of idols. So fight the minions of the devil. Lo! The devil's strategy is ever weak."[34] It is on verses like these that Al Qaeda bases its ideology and its call to kill Americans and their allies.

In order to fight a war against an ideology that demands killing in order for salvation we have to get to the core of that ideology and expose its fallacies. As was stated earlier, Al Qaeda errs on the side of violence in areas where the Quran can be interpreted in different ways. The United States has to do more work to show that Islam and the Quran can be interpreted in peaceful ways and that it is NOT purely a book of violence. We also have to encourage moderate Muslim groups to provide an outlet for the youths that are being recruited by Al Qaeda. If the only option to them is Al Qaeda's violence, then that is what they are going to follow. Finally, we need to "discredit the Al Qaeda inspired jihad as inconsistent with the writings of Islam and not a true Holy War."[35]

---

[33] Mneimneh, "Seven Years Later," 3.
[34] Quran 4:71.
[35] Drinkwine "Serpent In Our Garden," 43.

To accomplish this, the United States needs to work on its strategic communications efforts. This is not a new idea and people are working on it throughout the government. Unfortunately, more needs to be done to coordinate our efforts and ensure that they do not backfire on us. According to a study of public opinion done by WorldPublicOpinion.org between July and September of 2008, Al Qaeda is winning the fight. "There is a widespread majority belief that the United States seeks to weaken and divide the Islamic world… [and] just as majorities assume that the United States wants to weaken Islam, they see it as more than plausible that it is a U.S. goal to spread Christianity in the Middle East."[36]

CONCLUSION

A war of ideologies is not a simple battle. All aspects of a country's instruments of national power need to be utilized to their full extent. The only way to succeed is through the use of all diplomatic, information, military, and economic means. There might even be a fifth instrument of national power, spiritual power. This would make the commonly used acronym DIMES instead of DIME. From a purely military perspective, the western world will have to rely on its principles of war to be successful. Historically, the foes the United States has faced have had the same principles of war and used them in similar manners, but that is not the case in our battle with Al Qaeda. No longer are we facing an enemy that relies on the principles of war as first stated by Clausewitz, Jomini and other military theorists. Instead we face an elusive opponent with a networked structure that disperses itself and waits until the time is right for an attack. Understanding that Al Qaeda has different principles of war than those currently taught at western military colleges and civilian universities is the first step to successfully combating them.

---

[36] Steven R. Corman, "Getting Beat in the War of Ideas," *COMOPS Journal* 2009, 1.

Much research has been done on Al Qaeda and the various groups and organizations within it. This has been the case since well before the 9/11 attacks, but the numbers have increased greatly since then. Scholars and government officials have spent years trying to analyze the leadership of Al Qaeda to try and figure out where the next strike is going to occur or where the next battle will be in this global war we are fighting. Documents have been recovered that revealed what their strategic objectives are and what steps they are going to take in an attempt to accomplish these objectives. We have even found manuals that show how various cells have been organized. The problem is that Al Qaeda is a networked organization with no set structure that we can strike. Instead it is a group of cells that are networked and held together by a common ideology. It is only by attacking this networked structure and by discrediting the ideology that the United States and its allies can hope to gain the upper hand.

BIBLIOGRAPHY

Alger, John I. *The Quest for Victory.* Westport, CT: Greenwood Press, 1982.

Bell, Raymond E. "The Validity of the Principles of War." *Army* 57, no. 2 (Feb 2007): 20-22.

Breemer, Jan S. "Statistics, Real Estate, and the Principles of War: Why There is No Unified Theory of War." *Military Review* 86, no. 5 (Sep/Oct 2006): 84-89.

Corman, Steven R. "Getting Beat in the War of Ideas." COMOPS Journal, 2009.

Davis, John W. "Once and Future Principles of War." *The Officer* 82, no. 1 (Jan/Feb 2006): 47-50.

Drinkwine, Brian M. *The Serpent in Our Garden: Al Qa'ida and the Long War.* Strategic Studies Research Paper. Carlisle Barracks, PA: Strategic Studies Institute, 2009.

Dunlap, Charles J. Jr. "Neo-Strategicon: Modernized Principles of War for the 21st Century." *Military Review* 86, no. 2 (Mar/Apr 2006): 42-48.

Harmony Project, "AFGP-2002-600048," in *Harmony and Disharmony.*

Khan, Raza Muhammad. *Principles of War in the Twenty First Century.* Strategy Research Project. Carlisle Barracks, PA: U.S. Army War College, 1999.

Mattox, John Mark. "The Baby and the Bathwater: Changing Times or Changing Principles?" *Military Review* 88, no. 5 (Sep/Oct 2008): 5-9.

McIvor, Anthony D. ed., *Rethinking the Principles of War.* Annapolis, MD: Naval Institute Press, 2005.

Meilinger, Phillip S. "New Principles for New War." *Armed Forces Journal*, January 2009, 16-20.

Mneimneh, Hassan. "Seven Years Later: The Jihadist International." *Middle Eastern Outlook*, no. 6 (Sep 2008): American Enterprise Institute for Public Policy Research.

National Commission on Terrorist Attacks Upon the United States, *The 9/11 Commission Report.* New York: WW Norton & Company, 2004.

Pechurov, S.L. "Principles of War as Interpreted by Modern Military Science in the West." *Military Thought* 15, no.1 (2006): 135-142.

Piatt, Walter E. *Do the Principles of War Still Apply?* School of Advanced Military Studies Research Project. Ft Leavenworth, KS: U.S. Army Command and General Staff College, 1998.

The Holy Quran translated at www.sacred-texts.com accessed 24 April 2009.

Richardson, Don. *Secrets of the Koran: Revealing Insights into Islam's Holy Book.* Ventura, CA: Regal Books, 2003.

Ronfeldt, David. *Al-Qaeda and Its Affiliates: A Global Tribe Waging Segmental Warfare.* Rand Report # RP-1371, 2007.

Roots of Strategy Book 2. Harrisburg, PA: Stackpole Books, 1987.

Sageman, Marc. *Understanding Terror Networks.* Philadelphia, PA: University of Pennsylvania Press, 2004.

Sageman, Marc. *Leaderless Jihad: Terror Networks in the Twenty-First Century.* Philadelphia, PA: University of Pennsylvania Press, 2008.

Schneider, James J. "Agents of Change: Transforming the Principles of War for the 21st Century." *Army* 56, no. 7 (Jul 2006): 25-32.

Strategy and Policy Department, *In the Eyes of Your Enemy: An Al-Qaeda Compendium.*

U.S. Army, *Operations.* Field Manual (FM) 3-0, Washington D.C.: Department of the Army, February 2008.

Woods, Kevin M. *Iraqi Perspective Project: A View of Operation Iraqi Freedom from Saddam's Senior Leadership.* Suffolk, VA: Joint Center for Operational Analysis, 2006.

www.ingramcontent.com/pod-product-compliance
Lightning Source LLC
Chambersburg PA
CBHW081813280526
45789CB00008B/3118